PREFACE

The purpose of this work is to present the  do not present any specific version or a unique interp̃ am as it is, without sugarcoating, and we allow it to st nly one Islam and only one example of how it is to be ummad[p] (Peace be upon him).[1] Our intention is to provide enets of Islam as given in the Qur'an and as exemplified by the Prophet[p]. we also intend to address some of the commonly asked questions about Islam.

Despite the fact that over one-fifth of the world's population is Muslim, Islam is often misunderstood and misrepresented in contemporary Western societies. It is hoped that this work will help shed light on Islam as it was divinely communicated to Muhammad[p] and dispel any commonly held misconceptions that perpetuate prejudice and hatred. We write this booklet in the hope that people of all faiths will join us in making this a world of tolerance, kindness, understanding, and peace.

1. WHAT IS ISLAM?

The Arabic word Islam literally means "surrender" or "submission." Islam, as a faith, means total and sincere surrender to God so that one can live in peace and tranquility. Peace (Salam in Arabic, Shalom in Hebrew) is achieved through active obedience to the revealed commandments of God, for God is *The Just, The Peace*. (The *italicized* words throughout the text indicate either a verse from the Qur'an or one of the names and attributes of God.)

The name Islam[2] is universal in meaning. Islam is not named after a tribe of people or an individual, as Judaism is named after the tribe of Judah, Christianity after Christ, and Buddhism after Buddha. Islam is not a name chosen by human beings; it was divinely communicated from God. Islam is a global faith, not of the East or the West. Islam is a complete way of life, implying a total submission to God. One who surrenders his or her will to God, voluntarily,[3] is called a Muslim. It was not Muhammad[p] but Adam[p] who first brought Islam to humanity. Then, each Prophet and Messenger[p] came to exhort the people to a clear understanding of God's commandments. They offered teachings relevant to that time, until God chose the final Prophet, Muhammad[p], to come with the Last Testament referred to as the Qur'an.

Allah is an Arabic word, meaning *"The One and Only True God,"* the proper name of *The One* who created the heavens and the earth. **Arabic-speaking Jews and Christians also call God by the name *Allah*.** For a Muslim, *Allah* is the greatest and most inclusive of names for God, denoting *The One* who is adored in worship, *The One* who created all that exists.

2. MONOTHEISM

The concept of monotheism (known as tawheed in Arabic) is the single most important concept in Islam. Monotheism points to the first of the Ten Commandments, and in Islam everything is built upon the oneness of God. Islam calls humanity away from the worship of any part of creation to the worship of *The One and Only True God*.

---

1   The symbol (*[p]*) means "**P**eace and blessing be upon him (or them)." It is an Islamic tradition to offer blessings of **p**eace to all the Prophets and Messengers of God. To respect God's representatives is to respect God.

2   Some Muslims are uncomfortable calling Islam a "religion," as Islam is not an institutionalized faith. In Arabic Islam is referred to as a *Deen*, "Way of life." This is the same as early Christians who also called their faith "The Way."

3   "Voluntarily" in this sense means more than "not being coerced." It means surrendering to God without ulterior motives or reservations, and with genuine wholeheartedness.

No act of worship or devotion has any meaning or value if the concept of monotheism is in any way compromised.

Due to its importance, the concept of monotheism (divine unity and singularity) must be properly and fully understood. For ease of discussion, monotheism can be looked at from the following three perspectives:

   a. The **Oneness of God** in His Lordship (Omnipotence)
   b. The Devotion of All Worship to *The One* **God Alone**
   c. The Uniqueness and **Oneness of God** in His Names and Attributes

This breakdown is by no means the only way to approach the subject that **God is one and unique**, but it allows the topic to be easily analyzed and discussed. (Monotheism is the key to understanding Islam, and revisiting this concept is recommended.)

2*a*. THE ONENESS OF GOD IN HIS LORDSHIP (OMNIPOTENCE)

The oneness of God in His Lordship means that God, *The Originating Creator of the Heavens and the Earth*, has absolute and perfect mastery over the universe. **He alone is *The Creator* of all things**. He alone causes everything to happen. He is *The One* who provides all sustenance and who determines all life and death. He is *The Powerful*, *The Omnipotent*, absolutely perfect and free from any defect. No one shares in His dominion. None can resist His decree. He is *The One* who created each of us from a single cell and made us into what we are. He is *The One* who created over a hundred billion galaxies and every electron, neutron, and quark contained within them, keeping all that exists and all the laws of nature in perfect measure. Not a leaf falls from a tree without His permission. Everything is kept in a precise record.

He is far greater than our imagination. He is so powerful that for anything to be created He simply says "**Be**," and it is. He created time, space, and all the known and unknown worlds, yet He is not part of any of them. Most faiths recognize that *The Creator* of the universe is one, without partner. Islam includes the knowledge that God is not a part of His creation and none of His creation shares in His power.

In Islam, to believe that any of God's creation shares in His power or attributes is considered polytheism and disbelief. Examples of such false beliefs would be to consider that fortune-tellers or astrologers can predict the future; God, *The All Aware*, says that only He possesses the knowledge of the future. Only the Divine can give divine help. No being except God has the ability to give divine help or divine guidance. Belief that good luck charms and talismans have any power is a form of polytheism. These concepts are renounced in Islam.

2*b*. THE DEVOTION OF ALL WORSHIP TO THE ONE GOD ALONE

Only God, *The Appreciative*, is to be worshipped. This was proclaimed by all the Prophets and Messengers[p] of Islam who were sent by God throughout the ages, and is the core belief of Islam. God tells us that the purpose of the creation of humanity is to **worship Him alone**. The purpose of Islam is to call people away from the worship of creation and to direct them toward the worship of *The Creator* alone.

This is where Islam differs from other religions. Although most religions teach that there is a creator who created all that exists, they are rarely free of some form of polytheism (idolatry) with respect to worship. These religions either call on their adherents to worship other beings besides God (though usually placing these other gods on a lower level than the God who is *The Creator*), or they demand that their adherents call on other beings as intercessors between themselves and God.

All the Prophets and Messengers of God, from Adam[p] to Muhammad[p], called people **to worship God alone, without partner or intermediary**. This is the purest, simplest, most natural faith. Islam rejects the notion held by cultural anthropologists that the early religion of human beings was polytheism — which gradually evolved into monotheism. In fact, Muslims believe just the opposite, human cultures descended into idolatry during the intervals of time between the many Messengers of God. Even while the Messengers were among them, many people resisted their call and practiced idolatry despite their warnings. Subsequent Messengers were commissioned by God to bring people back to monotheism.

God created humans with an innate, natural inclination toward the worship of Him alone. Satan, on the other hand, does his utmost to get people to turn away from monotheism, enticing mankind to the worship of creation (idolatry). Most people have a tendency to focus their devotion on something they can visualize, something imaginable, even though they have an instinctive knowledge that *The Creator* of the universe is far greater than their imaginations. Throughout human history, God sent a succession of Prophets and Messengers to call the people back to the worship of *The One and Only True God*. Due to the allure of Satan, people repeatedly deviated to the worship of created beings (idolatry and polytheism).

God created human beings to worship Him alone. In Islam, the greatest possible sin is to worship anything or anyone other than God, even if the worshipper intends to get nearer to God by offering devotions to another being. God, *The Sufficient*, does not need intercessors or intermediaries. He hears all of our prayers and has complete knowledge of everything that happens.

At the same time, God does not need our worship, but He says that it is pleasing to Him. He is completely independent of all things. All creation is dependent upon Him. If every person in the world were to come together to worship only God, it would not benefit God in the least. It would not add an atom's weight to His majestic dominion. Conversely, if all creation abandoned the worship of God, it would not decrease His dominion in the least. By worshipping God, we benefit our own souls and fulfill the noble purpose for which we were created. God has no needs; He is The Eternal, The Absolute.

Worship is not just traditional religious ceremonies or practices. The concept of worship is inclusive. Changing a diaper, honoring and caring for one's parents, as well as picking up a piece of broken glass from the sidewalk — all can be forms of worship if they are done with the primary intent to please God. If any sort of gain, be it wealth, job, power, or recognition, becomes more important than pleasing God, even that is a form of polytheism.

2c. THE UNIQUENESS AND ONENESS OF GOD IN HIS NAMES AND ATTRIBUTES

The uniqueness and oneness of God in His names and attributes indicates that God does not **share** in the attributes of created beings, nor do they **share** in any of His. God is unique in every way. He cannot be limited in any way, for He is *The Creator* of everything. God, *The Most Great* says, "*God! None is worthy of worship but He, The Ever Living, The One who sustains and protects all that exists. Neither slumber nor sleep overtakes Him. To Him belongs whatever is in the heavens and whatever is on the earth. Who is he that can intercede with Him except with His permission? He knows what happens to them [His creatures] in this world, and what will happen to them in the Hereafter. And they will never encompass anything of His knowledge except that which He wills. The pedestal of His throne extends over the heavens and the earth, and*

He feels no fatigue in guarding and preserving them. And He is The Most High, The Supreme." [Qur'an 2:255]

In Islam it is forbidden to attribute to God characteristics of His creation. The only attributes that may be ascribed to God are the ones He revealed Himself in the Qur'an or those used by the Prophet*ᵖ* to describe Him. Many of God's names and attributes seem to have equivalents on the human level, but this is only a reflection of human language. God's attributes, like God Himself, are unlike anything in our experience. For instance, God has divine knowledge. Man has knowledge. God's knowledge however, is nothing at all like the knowledge of human beings. God's knowledge is unlimited (omniscient, *The All Knowing*). It is neither learned nor acquired. God's knowledge encompasses all things without experiencing increase or decrease. Human knowledge, on the other hand, is acquired and limited. It is constantly changing, increasing and decreasing, and subject to forgetfulness and error.

God, *The Irresistible*, has divine will. The human being also has a will. God's will always comes to pass. Like His divine knowledge, His will encompasses all things that God wants to come to pass in creation — past, present, and future. Human will, on the other hand, is merely an intention, a desire. It can only come to pass if God wills it to happen.

Human attributes cannot be ascribed to God. All human attributes are limited. **God has no gender**, weakness, or deficiency. God is beyond the human and creation attribute of gender. Here we have used the pronoun "He" only because there is no gender-neutral pronoun in English/Semitic languages, and it follows the conventions of English usage. When the royal "We" is used in the Qur'an to refer to God, it is for respect and in no way implies plurality. To ascribe to God attributes of created things is a form of polytheism. It is likewise a form of polytheism to ascribe to created things attributes that belong to God alone. For instance, anyone who believes that any other than God is *The All-Wise* or *All Powerful* has committed the sin of polytheism.

"*Blessed be the name of your Lord, full of majesty, bounty, and honor.*" [Qur'an 55:78]

3. THE SIX ARTICLES OF FAITH

There are certain tenets one must believe without any doubt in order to be considered a Muslim. These articles of faith are as follows:

    a. Belief in God
    b. Belief in His Angels
    c. Belief in His Books
    d. Belief in His Prophets and Messengers
    e. Belief in the Day of Judgment
    f. Belief in God's Divine Decree

3*a.* BELIEF IN GOD

Islam emphasizes that God is *The **One*** without partner, *The Encompassing* of all that exists, and He is unique in every way. Only God, The Most Benevolent, has the right to be worshipped.

3*b.* BELIEF IN HIS ANGELS

The angels are creations of God. God, *The Originator*, created them from light. They are powerful, and always do precisely as they are commanded by God.

God has revealed to us the names and the duties of some of the angels. A Muslim must believe in the existence of angels. Gabriel and Michael are among the angels mentioned in the Qur'an. For instance, it is Gabriel's duty to take God's revelation to the Prophets and Messengers*ᵖ*.

3c. BELIEF IN HIS BOOKS

Muslims believe in all of the original scriptures revealed by God to His Messengers[p]. A Muslim must believe in every scripture mentioned by God in the Qur'an. God, *The Giver*, revealed them and they were, in their original forms, the actual word of God. The scriptures God mentions in the Qur'an are as follows:

1. The original **Scrolls** as revealed to Abraham[p]
2. The original **Torah** as revealed to Moses[p]
3. The original **Psalms** as revealed to David[p]
4. The original **Injeel** (Gospel of Jesus) as revealed to Jesus[p][4]
5. The **Qur'an** as revealed to Muhammad[p] (which is still available in its original form)

Muslims do not consider the scriptures revealed before the Qur'an, which are presently in circulation in various editions and versions, to be an accurate representation of their original revealed form. According to the Qur'an, people have distorted these scriptures for their own worldly gain. These distortions have occurred in many different ways, such as additions or deletions of text or changes in the meaning or the language. These distortions were adopted over time and what remains is a mixture of the original divine text with manmade interpretation and contamination. Although Muslims believe in all the previous revealed books, the final means by which they judge different matters and seek ultimate guidance is sought through the Qur'an and the authentic traditions of the Prophet Muhammad[p].

3d. BELIEF IN HIS PROPHETS AND MESSENGERS[p]

The Prophets and Messengers[p] were individuals who received revelation from God and conveyed it to the people. They were sent to humanity to return people to monotheism, to serve as living practical examples of how to surrender to God, and to guide people to the path of salvation. None of the Prophets and Messengers[p] share in any part of God's divinity. They were merely human beings. It is forbidden for a Muslim to worship them or to use them as a conduit to God. A Muslim should never invoke them, make supplications to them, or seek God's mercy and forgiveness through or from them. Therefore, the term "Muhammadanism" is an insult and should never be applied to Muslims. Every single Prophet and Messenger taught that all such acts are polytheistic, and anyone who engages in them is outside the fold of Islam.

Throughout the ages, God, *The Bestower of Good*, has sent Prophets to people all over the world. A Muslim must believe in all of the Prophets and Messengers sent by God. God has mentioned some of them in the Qur'an. Among those mentioned by name[5] are Adam, Noah, Abraham, Moses, Jesus, and Muhammad. (Peace be upon them all)

All the Prophets and Messengers of God brought the teachings of Islam. Throughout history all monotheistic people who submitted to the will of God and followed God's revelation to the Prophets and Messengers of their time are considered Muslims. The entitlement to Abrahamic inheritance is acquired through one's adherence to Abraham's monotheistic faith and surrender to God, not by lineage alone. When Moses[p] came and proclaimed Prophethood, all those who truly followed him in monotheism were Muslims. Likewise, when Jesus[p] came and declared his Prophethood with clear signs and miracles, it was obligatory for everyone to accept him unconditionally if they were to be considered Muslims. All those who rejected Jesus[p]

---

4   The different gospels in today's Bible were written after the time of Jesus[p] by other authors. The Injeel mentioned in the Qur'an refers only to the revelations that came through Jesus[p], the son of Mary[p].

5   The Prophets mentioned in the Qur'an are: Adam, Enoch (Idris), Noah, Hud, Salih, Abraham, Lot, Ishmael, Isaac, Jacob, Joseph, Shu'ayb, Job, Moses, Aaron, Ezekiel, David, Solomon, Elias, Elisha, Jonah, Zachariya, John "The Baptist," Jesus, and Muhammad (Peace be upon them all).

became disbelievers in Islam because of that rejection.[6] Rejecting or disliking any of God's Messengers disqualifies one as Muslim. Muslims are required to love and respect all the Prophets and Messengers[P] of God who called upon humanity to worship *The Creator* alone without ascribing to Him any partner. All the Prophets and Messengers surrendered completely to God, which is Islam.

The Prophets, from Adam to Muhammad[P], were all brothers in faith. They all called people to the same truth. Different Messengers came with different sets of laws sent by God to guide and govern the people, but the essence of their teachings was the same. They all called people away from the worship of created things to the worship of *The Creator, The Supreme.*

In Islam, Muhammad[P] has the distinction of being God's final Messenger and the Seal of the Prophets. The reason for this is, first, because God completed His revelations to humanity and perfectly preserved them forever in the Qur'an, and second, His final Prophet and Messenger[P] led an exemplary life for the twenty-three years of his Prophethood, establishing clear guidelines for all generations to follow. God says in the Qur'an that no Prophet or Messenger will come after him. This is the reason Muhammad[P] is known as the Seal of the Prophets.[7] This means the divine law that was revealed and embodied in the teachings of Prophet Muhammad[P] is for all of humanity until the Day of Resurrection (Day of Judgment). To be a believer, it is obligatory to believe in Muhammad[P] and the laws that have been revealed through him, as well as in all the Prophets and Messengers of God who came before. Muhammad[P] and the Prophets and Messengers[P] before him also had to believe in, obey, and surrender to *The Almighty* God. Although Muslims believe in all the Prophets and Messengers[P] of God, they follow and emulate the teachings and example of the final Messenger Muhammad[P]. God *The Most Glorious*, states about Muhammad[P], "*And We have not sent you, but as a mercy to the worlds.*" [Qur'an 21:107]

3e. BELIEF IN THE DAY OF JUDGMENT

Muslims must believe, without any doubt, in the Day of Judgment and the physical resurrection when the body will be recreated and the soul will surely be reunited with the body by God's unlimited power. Just as God, *The Gatherer of Mankind*, created us the first time, He is surely *The Resurrector* who will bring us forth from death to stand in perfect judgment before Him. After the Day of Judgment, death will no longer be, and our existence will be forever. The Day of Judgment is when each and every individual will stand before *The Creator* and be questioned about his or her deeds. On that momentous day, we will each see in detail the results of even the smallest good and the smallest evil we have set forth in this life. On that day, lying and deception will no longer be possible. The ultimate reward is Paradise and the penalty is Hell. Heaven and Hell are literal places that actually exist. They are not symbols or metaphors.

God, *The Recognizer and Rewarder of Good*, describes Paradise (Heavenly garden) as a wonderful place of pleasure, filled with amazing eternal gardens with rivers flowing beneath. In Paradise, no hot or cold, no disease, fatigue, or evil will exist. God, *The Giver of Security*, will remove disease from the heart and body of its inhabitants, and everything one wishes for will be granted. It will be said to those who enter Paradise: This Paradise you have inherited as a result of God's mercy and your good

---

6   God revealed to Muhammad[P], "*The same religion has He established for you as that which He enjoined on Noah, that which We have sent by inspiration to thee, and that which We enjoined on Abraham, Moses, and Jesus: Namely, that you should remain steadfast in religion, and make no divisions therein. To those who worship other things than God, hard is the [way] to which you call them. God chooses to Himself those whom He pleases, and guides to Himself those who turn to Him.*" [Qur'an 42:13]

7   Some Muslims refer to the following Biblical verses as the foretelling of the Prophet Muhammad[P]: [Deut. 18:15, 18:18; John 1:19 – 21, 14:16, 14:17, 15:26, 16:7 – 8, 16:12 – 13]

deeds. The greatest of pleasures in the Hereafter will be the believers' ability to see the face of God, *The Most High*. Being a Muslim in and of itself does not assure Paradise unless one dies in a state of Islam — submission to *The One* God alone.

God, *The Reckoner*, describes Hell as an eternally horrible place, beyond imagination, a fire whose fuel is men and stone. When stern angels place people in Hell, they will say, "*This is that which you used to deny.*" [Qur'an 83:17] We believe God is *The Most Compassionate* and *The Most Merciful*; however, He is also severe in His punishment to those who deserve it.

God's infinite justice is absolute and perfect. On the Day of Judgment, all deeds will be revealed and everyone will be justly treated. We will not enter Paradise because of our deeds alone, but by God's mercy.

3f. BELIEF IN DIVINE DECREE

God, in His timelessness, knows everything that goes on in His creation. From the perspective of temporal beings like us, this means that God, *The Ever Watching*, knows everything that happened in the past, everything that is now taking place, and everything that will happen in the future. God's divine knowledge is perfect. God is *The All Knowing*, and all that He knows will come to pass.

God, *The Subduer*, Has absolute sovereignty over His creation. Everything that exists within His creation and every event that occurs is a direct result of His creating it. Nothing happens in creation except by His power, His will, and His knowledge.

4. THE FREE WILL OF THE HUMAN BEING

An important aspect of Islam is that every human being has the free will to choose between right and wrong. God, *The Giver*, has honored humanity with this great gift. It comes with heavy responsibility, and on the Day of Judgment, we will be accountable for our use of this gift.

Human free will does not in any way contradict the fact that God, *The Witness*, knows everything that will ever occur in creation. Someone might ask, "If God knows that I am going to commit a sin tomorrow, then it is unavoidable that I do so because God's knowledge is infallible, and what God knows will come to pass." God's knowledge of this person's decision does not mean that he or she is being forced to make that decision.

Human free will does not in any way contradict God's absolute sovereignty over everything in creation. Neither does it contradict the fact that nothing happens in creation except what God wills. Some might say, "Therefore, I have no free will. My free will is but an illusion." On the contrary, God created within each of us the ability to formulate an intention. God wants us to be able to make our own choices. When a person makes a choice, God, by His divine will, creates the actions and circumstances that allow the person's intention to be carried out. It is God's will that human beings have free will. God is not always pleased with the decisions people make, but He wants them to be able to make these decisions by their own free choice. An example of this is a person's will to do a good deed. The good deed may never be carried out, but God may reward the person for his or her intention to do a good deed. If the good deed comes to pass, God's will allowed it to take place, and God will reward both the intention and the action. In other words, God, *The Judge*, may reward you for good deeds willed but not carried out; however, He does not punish people for bad intentions not acted upon.

5. THERE IS NO COMPULSION IN RELIGION

From this emphasis on free will, it follows that Islam can only be accepted by free choice. The purpose of human life is to **worship God of one's own free will**. Therefore, matters of faith have value **only** if they are accepted on the basis of freedom of choice. If a person is coerced into accepting any religion, that acceptance is false and has no value. God, *The Gentle,* says, *"**There is no compulsion in religion**. Truth stands out clear from error: whoever rejects evil and believes in God has grasped the most trustworthy handhold that never breaks. And God hears and knows all things."* [Qur'an 2:256]

6. THE FIVE PILLARS OF ISLAM

There are five obligatory acts of worship that every Muslim must dutifully carry out. Failure to do so is a grave sin. The edifice of Islam rests upon these five pillars. One cannot be considered a Muslim if he or she denies that any one of these acts is obligatory.

The five obligations of Muslims are as follows:
> *a.* The declaration of faith, to **"Testify that there is no deity except God, and that Muhammad is His Messenger"** (Shahadah)
> *b.* To **pray** five times a day (Salah)
> *c.* To pay the yearly **alms** (Zakah)
> *d.* To **fast** during the month of Ramadan (Sawm)
> *e.* To make the **pilgrimage** to Makkah (Hajj)

6a. THE DECLARATION OF FAITH (SHAHADAH)

It is obligatory for every person intending to enter Islam to believe and to say, "**I testify that there is no deity except God, and that Muhammad is His Messenger**." With this simple, important, and powerful declaration, a person is considered a Muslim. There is no initiation into the fold of Islam.

The concepts within the testimony of faith can be explained by analyzing each of three parts within the testimony. The first part "**No deity…**" is a negation of polytheism.[8] **It is a negation of the existence of any deity other than God, or any entity that shares in any of the divine attributes of God**. The second part "**…except God**" is an affirmation of monotheism. **God is the only one worthy of worship**.

"**Muhammad is God's Messenger**" is the third part of the declaration of faith. It is an affirmation of the Prophethood of Muhammad[p] as the final Prophet and Messenger of God.[9] This requires the unconditional acceptance of the Qur'an and the authentic sayings and traditions of Muhammad[p].

By believing and saying the testimony of faith, a person rejects all false objects of worship and asserts that God is the only one to be worshipped. God is without equal or partner. God promises that once a person affirms and sincerely says, "**I testify that there is no deity except God, and that Muhammad is His Messenger**," all of his or her previous sins are forgiven. One's previous good deeds may also be rewarded by God, *The Most Forgiving.*

---

8   This negation means that nothing is to be worshipped except God, nothing has divinity except God, none share the attributes of God, and none can be the creator or sustainer of creation except God, who is without equal or partner.

9   One may ask, "If Islam teaches that all the Prophets and Messengers are equal, then why does the testimony of faith only affirm the Prophethood of Muhammad without mentioning the other Prophets?" It must be understood that anyone who affirms the Prophethood of Muhammad[p] is acknowledging all the Prophets and Messengers[p] of God that came before him. If one were to testify for example, that, "There is no deity except God, and Moses is the Messenger of God," this does not necessitate the person's acceptance of the Prophets and Messengers that followed Moses[p], such as Jesus[p] or Muhammad[p].

6b. PRAYING FIVE TIMES A DAY (SALAH)

It is required for every Muslim to perform five obligatory prayers a day. A Muslim turns toward Makkah (Mecca) when performing these prayers, facing the first house built for the worship of *The One* God. This house is called the Ka`bah, an empty cube-like structure which is located in what is now Saudi Arabia. It was erected by Abraham[p] and his son Ishmael[p] for the worship of *The One and Only True God.*

One must remember that Islam does not have any sacred relics or symbols. We are not worshipping the Ka`bah; we simply worship God while facing the Ka`bah. Facing the Ka`bah to pray unifies the worshippers in their prayer to *The One* God. Anyone who worships the Ka`bah or any other created thing would be considered an idol worshipper. To put it plainly, the building materials that make up this house are no more sacred than any other building materials.

These prayers take place throughout the day and night, and are a constant reminder of a person's duty and surrender to God. The prayers are a direct link between the worshipper and God. It is a chance to turn to God in worship, to give thanks, to ask for forgiveness, and to ask for His guidance and mercy.

A Muslim may voluntarily perform prayers more often. Prayers, in the general sense of supplication, can be offered practically at any time or place.

6c. PAYING THE YEARLY ALMS (ZAKAH)

It is a religious duty for every Muslim who is prosperous enough to accumulate and retain a sufficient amount of savings to give a portion of his or her wealth to the needy each year. These alms are called Zakah in Arabic, which literally means "purification." All things belong to God, *The Most Merciful*, and wealth is held in trust by human beings. Paying these alms is a way for people who are financially able to purify the ethically gained wealth that God has bestowed upon them. In addition, it is a means to directly distribute wealth throughout society and help the poor and needy. Zakah (alms) also purifies the soul of the giver, reduces greed, and strengthens compassion and generosity among humanity. The basic rate of these alms is two and a half percent of the wealth that has been held in savings for an entire year. These alms are levied on savings, not income.

6d. FASTING DURING RAMADAN (SAWM)

A physically able adult Muslim must fast during the lunar month of Ramadan. This month is significant because the first revelations of the Qur'an to Muhammad[p] occurred during this month. Since a year in the lunar calendar is eleven days shorter than the solar calendar, the month of Ramadan gradually passes through all seasons of the year. Just as almsgiving is a form of wealth purification, fasting is a form of self-purification. Fasting begins at dawn and ends at sunset, local time. During daylight hours, a fasting person must abstain from food, drink, and marital sexual intercourse.[10] These activities are permissible from sunset to the following dawn. Fasting teaches self-control and patience. Like prayer, fasting is a way of turning to God in sincere worship. The two holidays for Muslims are Eid Al-Fitr which is celebrated at the end of Ramadan, and Eid Al-Adha which is celebrated at the end of hajj. Fasting reminds us of the conditions of the needy and gives us appreciation for the simple blessings we often take for granted, such as drinking a glass of pure water or eating food at will.

6e. MAKING THE PILGRIMAGE TO MAKKAH (HAJJ)

Every Muslim is to make the pilgrimage to the Ka`bah, in Makkah, once in a lifetime if he or she has the ability and means to do so. Muslims from all over the world

---

10   Islam requires chastity and forbids any premarital sexual relationships.

gather together for the purpose of worshipping and pleasing God alone. Millions of pilgrims visit the Ka`bah and perform hajj annually.

The rite of hajj originated from the Prophet Abraham[p] and was restored by Muhammad[p]. The pilgrimage to Makkah compels the pilgrims to break down the racial, economic, and social barriers that may still plague their societies. It also invites each pilgrim to practice patience, self-restraint, and piety. The pilgrims wear simple garments that strip away the distinctions of class and culture. Each of these obligatory acts of worship keeps the remembrance of God alive and reminds all Muslims that from God we come and to God we will all return.

7. THE QUR'AN

The Qur'an is the final, infallible, direct, and complete record of the exact words of God, brought down by the angel Gabriel[11] and firmly implanted in the heart of His final Prophet and Messenger, Muhammad[p]. The Qur'an was learned and memorized by many of Muhammad's[p] companions and passed down to us via meticulous oral (primary) and written (secondary) preservation through the centuries.

The books that came before the Qur'an through God's Prophets and Messengers[p] were also sent by God. By revealing the Qur'an, God's message was restored and clarified. The Qur'an is unique in a number of ways. God, *The Guardian*, has perfectly preserved the Qur'an and guaranteed it from corruption until the end of time. The Qur'an is regarded, not just by Muslims but also by historians of religion, as the most authentic religious text among the world's religions.[12] None of the other revealed books have reached us in their original form or language. Some of them, like the scrolls that were revealed through Abraham[p], have not reached us at all. Over the course of time, parts of other scriptures were rewritten and some parts removed, distorting their message.

God did not allow this contamination to happen to the Qur'an because it is His **final book** for all of humanity until the Day of Judgment. No new Prophet or Messenger is going to be sent. If God had not protected the Qur'an, it would have never reached us in its original pure form. For this reason, God did not entrust human beings with preserving the Qur'an.[13]

Divine preservation of the earlier scriptures was not as critical because God continued to send a succession of Prophets and Messengers to the people. The law as embodied in these older scriptures was not in its final complete form. By God's order, Jesus[p] came with modifications to the law, for instance, making lawful some things that had previously been unlawful without making any changes to the core concept of monotheism.

Another unique quality of the Qur'an is that it is an amazing miracle in and of itself. A miracle is a phenomenon that goes against the natural order of things and clearly demonstrates the direct intervention of God *The Almighty*.

All the Prophets and Messengers brought miracles from God that clearly demonstrated the truthfulness of their claim to Prophethood. Abraham[p] survived being thrown into a blazing fire without being harmed. Moses[p] raised his staff and the sea

---

11   It is taught in Islam that "the spirit of the Holy One" is the angel Gabriel, who should never be worshipped. (Belief in the trinity clearly contradicts the core principle of the Islamic faith — monotheism.)

12   See Joseph van Ess, "Muhammad and the Qur'an: Prophecy and Revelation" in Christianity and the World Religions: Paths to Dialogue with Islam, Hinduism, and Buddhism, edited by Hans Kung (Garden City, NY: Doubleday & Co., 1986); and Michael Sells, Approaching the Qur'an: The Early Revelations (Ashland, OR: White Cloud Press, 1999).

13   The Qur'an consists of 114 chapters and is a single book, unlike the various current versions of the Bible. Protestant Christians count 66 books in their version and Roman Catholic Christians count 72 books. There are even more books in other versions.

parted for him by God's mercy. Jesus[p], the son of Mary, touched the dead and terminally ill and restored them to life and full health by the permission of God. All of these miracles revealed the legitimacy and validity of the Prophets and Messengers, but these miracles could only be witnessed by the people who were actually there at that time.

While the Prophethood of Muhammad[p] was similarly attested to by various miraculous occurrences, by far the most important of all is the Glorious Qur'an. God challenges all those who doubt the authenticity of the Qur'an to produce a single chapter similar to a chapter of the Qur'an. (It should be pointed out that the smallest chapter of the Qur'an is composed of just three short verses.) This has never been accomplished though there have been many people throughout history who would have loved to discredit the Qur'an and do away with Islam. God's challenge remains open until the Day of Judgment. One of the Qur'an's miracles is that it is the pinnacle of literary excellence. It is the most eloquent Arabic prose in existence. It has a style like no other work in the Arabic language, a style that is inimitable. The Qur'an is for all people and is available to us in its original, living language, Arabic, which is still greatly used throughout the world by millions of people. The original texts of many other religious books have been lost over time and were originally written in languages that are no longer commonly spoken.

Not a single word in the Qur'an is the word of Muhammad[p], but all are the words of God. Muhammad[p] actually did not know how to read or write. He recited the Qur'an precisely as it was revealed to him by the angel Gabriel, while his companions, at his direction, recorded it in writing and memorized it. **The Qur'an is the direct word of God**. Therefore, the Qur'an is the only book we have today that is known to be authored by God alone. There are no other versions of the Qur'an. Although there are many translations of the meaning of the Qur'an, they are not nearly as magnificent and beautiful as the Qur'an's plain Arabic text. Here is a sample of the Qur'an, chapter 112 of the English translation of it's meaning:

"*In the name of God, The Most Gracious, The Most Merciful*
1. Say: He is God, The One and Only; 2. God, The Eternal, Absolute;
3. He begets not, nor was He begotten; 4. And there is none comparable unto Him."

8. THE PROPHET MUHAMMAD[p] AND HIS SUNNAH

Muhammad[p] was born in the year 570 CE from the honorable lineage of the two great Prophets of God, Abraham[p] and his firstborn son, Ishmael[p]. Muhammad[p] grew up with the title of **The Trustworthy**. At the age of forty, Muhammad[p] was chosen by God to be His last Prophet and Messenger.

The Sunnah refers to the sayings, actions, and tacit approvals of the Prophet Muhammad[p]. The reports and narrations about the Sunnah are known as Hadith, and are collected in well-known books. Like the Qur'an, the Sunnah is inspired by revelation from God through the Prophet Muhammad[p]. Unlike the Qur'an, it is not the direct, literal word of God. The teachings came from God (divine revelation) and the words were from the Prophet Muhammad[p] (an example for humanity). The Sunnah was also meticulously preserved.

It is obligatory for Muslims to follow the Sunnah of the Prophet Muhammad[p]. In the Qur'an, God orders the believers to obey the Messenger (His representative). God says, "*Obey God, and obey the Messenger.*" [Qur'an 4:59]

The purpose of life is to serve and obey God. This is achieved through following the teachings and practices of the Prophet[p]. God says, "*You have indeed in the Messenger of God a beautiful pattern [of conduct] for anyone whose hope is in God and the final day, and who engages much in the praise of God."* [Qur'an 33:21]

The Prophet[p] showed Muslims how to perform all aspects of worship. He died at the age of 63 (in the year 632 CE) and was buried at his home in the city of Medina (Yathrib). He always greeted and parted from his companions with salutations and invocations of peace, which is recommended for all Muslims. Within a century, Islam spanned three continents, from China across Asia, throughout Africa, and into Spain in Europe.

9. THE DANGERS OF INNOVATIONS IN ISLAM (BID'AH)

God ordered Muslims not to divide themselves into sects. Innovations and divisions in matters of religion and worship within Islam are considered to be contamination, error, and deviation. Earlier heinous deviations from monotheism, such as worshipping creation, resulted in condemnation by God. (However, innovations in other matters, such as science and technology to improve life, are greatly encouraged.) God, *The Most Compassionate*, has told us through His last Prophet Muhammad[p], when Muhammad[p] was nearing the end of his life, that He had completed the religion of Islam. Muslims must recognize that any change in matters of worship is strictly forbidden. No change introduced by humankind, who is under the influence of Satan, could ever add anything positive and would only contribute to the degradation of the completed and perfected religion established by God. All innovations in matters of religion lead to straying, and all straying leads to hellfire. People must not allow any deviation (addition or deletion), even as small as one degree, in matters of worship.[14] If any changes are allowed, those deviations will be compounded by future generations, and the result will be another **manmade religion**, not the Islam as it was perfected by God, *The Truth*. To build a faith using a "shopping cart" approach or the blind following of any religious leader is inadmissible.

The changing of God's laws is forbidden in Islam. God condemns religious leaders who alter divine principles. One who attempts to make changes places him or herself on the same level with God, committing polytheism. An example of this would be to make the killing of innocents lawful. The laws of God are perfect and do not need to be "modernized" by anyone. God allows us the freedom to obey or disobey Him by choosing to follow His faith or to follow our own desires. However, He forbids us to change His religious principles.

(It is interesting to note that the crescent moon is not representative of the religion of Islam, as the Prophet Muhammad[p] never used or mentioned it. It was a pagan symbol and an innovation brought about by later generations as a political symbol. Sadly, it is commonly adopted and mistaken as an Islamic symbol.)

10. THE STORY OF ADAM AND EVE

The story of Adam and Eve is told in the Qur'an. Although it is similar in many ways to what is found in the surviving remnants of the previous scriptures, some important principles differ.

God announced to the angels that He was placing a new specie on earth. God created Adam[p], fashioning him from clay. He breathed the soul into Adam[p], taught him the names of all things, and created from the same soul his wife, Eve. God allowed them to dwell in Paradise with free will. God said to the angels, "Bow down to Adam" (They

---

14   Islam teaches that for an act of **worship** to be accepted by God it must fulfill two conditions: The **intention** must be first and foremost to please God, and the act must be done **according to the Sunnah** of the Prophet Muhammad[p].

did so in a form of respect, not worship). Satan was present among the angels, though he was not one of them. He was of the jinn,[15] a race of beings possessing free will that God created before Adam[p] from a smokeless flame of fire. When God ordered the angels and those in their company to bow down to Adam[p], they all did so except Satan, who refused out of pride and arrogance, claiming to be better than Adam[p] because he was created from fire, whereas Adam[p] was created from clay. Indeed, Satan was the first racist.

Satan fell from God's grace. God, *The Reckoner*, condemned him for his disobedience, but Satan, the accursed, asked God to give him respite until the Day of Judgment (resurrection), so he could make Adam[p] and his descendants unworthy. Satan said, "Verily I will mislead them and surely I will arouse in them vain desires." God granted him this respite as a trial for humanity. God knows what Satan knows not. It is important to note that there is no way Satan could ever "war" with God, because just like everything else, he is God's creation. Satan exists only by God's will; he is completely under God's power. If God did not want Satan or his helpers to exist, they would not be able to remain in existence for even a moment.

Islam does not give Satan any share of God's divinity. It does not attribute to him any godlike or divine qualities. Islam rejects the notion that Satan went to war with God and took a third of the hosts of Heaven with him. Satan is an avowed enemy of humanity, but he is merely a creature, absolutely dependent upon God for his very existence.

Though prideful, accursed, and fallen from the grace of God, Satan serves a purpose. God wanted humans to have free choice between right and wrong. He granted human beings an innate ability to recognize *The Creator* and turn to Him. The human being is considered to be originally good by nature, born pure in the state of Islam (submission). Satan and his hosts order evil and oppose good, seeking to misguide humanity, his avowed enemy, into evil and idolatry, away from monotheism, righteousness, and the path of God. God, *The All Wise*, invites Muslims to **enjoin good and forbid evil**. Because we exercise free will, by resisting the temptation of Satan, humans can attain a great level of honor.

The following is a summary of the trial of Adam and Eve in Paradise: They enjoyed perfect freedom and happiness in Paradise. God told them to eat of the fruits of the Garden with pleasure and delight as they pleased. He forbade them from approaching one tree, and warned them that if they did, they will both be of the wrongdoers. Satan came and deceived them, saying that God only forbade them from eating of that tree because it would make them immortal or they would become like the angels. They were thus deceived by Satan and ate of the tree.

Adam and Eve felt shame. They turned to God in sincere repentance and God, *The All-Forgiving*, *The Most Gracious*, *The Most Merciful*, forgave them. Islam clearly rejects the concept of original sin, or the notion that all humans are born sinners because of the actions of Adam. No human shall ever bear the burden of another (for God is *The Just*). Every human being is responsible for his or her actions and is born as a Muslim, pure and free from sin. It is important to note that Islam does not place the blame on Eve. Both Adam and Eve had free will. Both of them ate of the tree. Their sin and disobedience was a joint venture. Islam rejects the idea that women are wicked temptresses or cursed with the burden of menstruation and pain of childbirth due to the sin of Eve.

---

15   The jinn were created before Adam; they have free will. Disobedient jinns are demons. They live here with us in some manner by which they can see us but we cannot see them unless they choose to make themselves appear. Sorcery, which is forbidden in Islam, is also performed through them.

God removed Adam and Eve from Paradise and made them dwell on earth. God had earlier said to the angels that He was placing a new being on earth. Earth is where God, from the time of creation, in His timeless knowledge, wanted us to be.

11. JESUS[p]

Jesus[p] was a Prophet and Messenger of God. He called to the oneness of God. He never claimed divinity for himself, **nor did he ever ask to be worshipped**.

He was born of a virgin. This was one of the many miracles regarding Jesus[p] given by God. Jesus[p] was born without a father. God says in the Qur'an, "*Truly the likeness of Jesus with God is as the likeness of Adam. He created him of dust and then said to him 'Be!' and he was.*" [Qur'an 3:59] God created Jesus[p] as He created everything else in existence. Jesus[p], Adam and Eve were all uniquely created: Jesus[p] was created without a father; Adam and Eve were created without a father or a mother. The rest of us were all created with a mother and a father. To believe that Jesus[p] is the begotten son of God or that God has any relatives such as a father, mother, son, or daughter, gives the attribute of procreation to *The Creator*.[16] Muslims believe this to be polytheism and it is absolutely forbidden in Islam. Likewise, giving attributes of *The Creator* to His creation is a great sin, which in Islam is clearly in opposition to monotheism. This belief is in contradiction to the teachings of all the Prophets and Messengers[p] of God.[17] God is beyond any created or human attributes. Jesus[p] is the Messiah, the Christ, the word of God, the anointed one, sent by *The Most Merciful* God as a Prophet and Messenger.

God also informs us that Jesus[p], the son of Mary, is not dead, and that He raised Jesus[p] up to Him. Muslims believe that the return of Jesus[p] will be a sign of the Last Days. When Jesus[p] returns, he will not come in the capacity of a Prophet and Messenger to bring new revelations. Rather, he will be the commander of the faithful and will destroy the antichrist, who will have brought to the earth enormous trials and evil. Jesus[p] will follow the final manifestation of the law that was revealed to Muhammad[p].

12. SIN AND REPENTANCE

Sin is willfully and knowingly disobeying God. The greatest of all sins is polytheism, though any intentional violation of the commandments of God is a sinful act. God, *The Preventer*, has prohibited a number of things that are harmful to the individual or to society. Murder, assault, theft, fraud, usury (footnote 18), fornication, adultery, sorcery (footnote 15), consumption of alcohol, eating pork, and the use of illicit drugs are all examples of sinful acts.

Islam rejects the doctrine of original sin. No soul shall bear the burden of another, as this would be a great injustice because God, *The Most Merciful*, is *The Just*. Each of us is accountable before God, *The All Seeing*, for our own deeds. However, if one person

---

16   It was in the ancient city of Nicea (which was located in modern-day Turkey approximately 700 miles or 1100 km NNW of Jerusalem near the eastern Roman capitol) that the First Council of Nicea convened, 325 years after the birth of Jesus[p]. It was at this council that Jesus[p] was declared by the majority of the council members to be divine rather than God's Prophet and Messenger. The concept of the trinity was established by declaring that Jesus[p] was the same as and equal to God. This is in direct opposition to the Abrahamic principles of monotheism, which Jesus[p] himself called people to and affirmed.

Islam teaches that the conception of Jesus[p] occurred when the angel Gabriel was ordered by God to bring Mary glad tidings of a son that would be born from her as a guide and mercy for humanity. She asked how that could be when no man had ever touched her. Gabriel answered, "If God says, '**Be**,' it is." For this reason, Jesus[p], the son of Mary, is at times called "Word of God." The "Word" is God's statement, "**Be**."

17   Even though Christians and Jews may violate some of the monotheistic tenets of their original Abrahamic faith, Islam refers to them respectfully as the "People of the Book." They are referred to in this way because they have received revealed laws and scriptures from God and do recognize some of His Prophets.

encourages another to commit a sin, both are punishable. One of them deserves punishment for actually committing the sin; the other deserves punishment for encouraging it.

When a person commits a sin, he or she is deserving of God's punishment. Fortunately, God is *The Most Compassionate* and *The Oft-Forgiving*. God acts out of infinite knowledge and justice. Muslims do not believe that Jesus[p], the son of Mary, had to die for the sins of mankind. God, *The Most Compassionate*, forgives whomever He chooses. To believe that it was necessary for Jesus[p] to suffer and die in order to have our sins forgiven denies God's infinite power and justice. God is unlimited in His mercy.

God, *The Answerer*, promises us that He will forgive us if we turn to Him in sincere repentance. Repentance is a serious matter. It is the way a person can attain salvation by the mercy of God. Repentance cannot be taken lightly. Sincere repentance has the following conditions:

1. The person must **recognize** and acknowledge that he or she has committed a sin and must truly regret having done so.
2. The person must humbly **turn to God for forgiveness**.
3. The person must have a sincere **resolve** not to commit the sin again.
4. If the sin caused harm to someone else, the person must make every possible attempt to **remedy** the harm.

This does not mean that if the person returns to the same sin in the future, his or her former repentance is annulled. What is needed is a serious commitment in the heart not to sin again. Because we do not know what the future holds, the door to repentance is always open. God, *The Oft-Pardoning*, is pleased when the children of Adam turn to Him for His abundant forgiveness. Repentance is a form of worship.

No one can forgive sins except God. It is forbidden for a Muslim to seek divine forgiveness for sin through or by turning to anyone else, as Muslims believe this would be considered polytheism.

13. ORGANIZATIONAL STRUCTURE OF ISLAM

Islam places emphasis on the individual's relationship with God. The framework for this relationship follows the guidelines set out by the Qur'an and Sunnah. This relationship, in turn, defines a Muslim's relations with everyone, which brings about justice, organization, and social harmony.

The Qur'an says, "*Verily the most honorable of you with God are the most pious among you.*" [Qur'an 49:13] The wise, the pious, the knowledgeable in Islam, and the true in practice are Islam's natural leaders.

Islam is not specific as to who can become a scholar. Anyone with enough intelligence, study, and determination can strive to become a scholar, but not everyone will have the time and resources to do so. All people should strive to learn as much as possible, while recognizing that God is *The One*, *The Bestower* of knowledge and understanding.

The scholar plays a critical role in Muslim society. He or she devotes years to the study of Islam. Scholars cannot forgive sins, bless people, or change the law of God. They impart the information they have acquired by reference to the Qur'an and Sunnah; by the nobility of their character they inspire others to be better.

Some have used the word "cleric" to describe a Muslim scholar. This is a misnomer. There is no formal clergy, no ordaining body, and no hierarchy. The relationship between the individual and God is a direct one. No one besides God can declare what is lawful and what is sinful. No created being can bless another. Each individual is directly accountable to his or her Lord and Creator.

One visiting a mosque may see a person leading the congregational prayers. Whenever Muslims pray together, they must select one individual to stand in front and lead the others in prayer so that all might pray in unity and harmony. It is best to select a person who has the most knowledge of the Qur'an and Islam. This person is called Imam, which literally means "the one who is leading." At midday on Fridays there is a special congregational prayer. All Muslim men are required to attend; it is voluntary for women. This weekly prayer is preceded by a short sermon. The one who gives this sermon should be the best available in terms of his deep understanding of Islamic principles.

14. ISLAMIC LAW

Islamic law is derived only from the Qur'an and the Sunnah of the Prophet Muhammad[p]. Like the Qur'an, the Sunnah is inspired by revelation from God. Islamic law covers all aspects of life. It deals with how to worship God and how to deal with others. God commands the believers to do certain things and bans them from doing others. God alone, *The All Knowing*, *The Just*, has the right to make some things lawful and other things sinful and forbidden. An Islamic society can legislate any laws for the improvement of life (e.g., traffic laws) as long as they are not in contradiction to Islamic law. God, *The Guide* and *The Director*, encourages some things without commanding them and discourages some behaviors without prohibiting them outright. All of these injunctions, taken together, form the law of Islam. When we add the fact that there are issues that Islamic law considers simply permissible, this makes five basic rulings for every human action:

1. **Obligatory** *2.* **Encouraged** *3.* **Permitted** *4.* **Discouraged** *5.* **Forbidden**

Islamic law is of divine origin. The reason we obey these laws is because God commands us to do so. We are encouraged to understand the wisdom behind the law, yet we are expected to obey even when we do not fully understand the reasons why. Understanding is an added gift. For example, eating pork is forbidden because God said so. We refrain from eating it for that reason, and not because we also happen to know scientifically that it contains unique diseases and is the least healthy meat. Even if scientists were able to genetically breed pigs to be a disease-free and most nutritious food, it would still be forbidden to eat pork. (However, someone may eat pork to save his or her life if there are no other options left, and there would be no sin in doing so.)

The sources of Islamic law are the Qur'an and Sunnah. God considers it polytheism to allow a religious leader to change God's command by making lawful what God has made forbidden, or by making forbidden what God has made lawful.[18] In this world, God alone determines what is good and what is sinful. In the Hereafter, God alone has the power and wisdom to reward those who do good and punish those who do evil.

15. THE ISLAMIC DRESS CODE

Islam promotes modesty and seeks to minimize vice and immorality in society. One of the ways it does so is by requiring modest dress. Islam sets the standards of decency for both men and women.

In most Western countries there are laws defining what is decent. This usually amounts to the male having to cover his genitals and the female having to cover her

---

18   Charging any amount of interest on a loan, or usury, was originally forbidden in Judaism, Christianity, and Islam. However, Christians in Europe from the time of the Middle Ages gradually changed this prohibition. Today, even "Islamic countries" have allowed this gross violation of God's law.

genitals and her breasts. If this minimum requirement is not met, the most a person can be charged with is indecent exposure. The reason cited for the difference in required clothing between men and women in this matter is the difference in their anatomies.

Islam prescribes a more conservative minimum dress code for both men and women. In Islam, both men and women are expected to dress simply, modestly, and with dignity. A man must always be covered in loose and unrevealing clothing from his navel to his knee. This is the absolute minimum covering required. He must never, for example, go out in public wearing a short bathing suit. When leaving the home, a Muslim woman must at least cover her hair and body in loose and unrevealing clothing, obscuring the details of her body from the public; some also choose to cover their face and hands. The wisdom behind this dress code is to minimize sexual enticement and degradation in society as much as possible for both men and women. Obeying this dress code is a form of obedience to God. Islam forbids any sex appeal and physical allurement outside of marriage. In contrast, Islam encourages sex appeal and physical attraction for both men and women within the privacy between married couples.

Some Western observers have assumed that the head covering of a woman is meant to show her inferiority to men. This could not be further from the truth. In Islam, a woman who dresses this way commands respect, and through her modesty rejects sexual servitude. The message that the woman gives when she wears Islamic dress in society is this: "Respect me for who I am. I am not a sex object."

Islam teaches that the consequences of immodesty fall not only on the individual but also upon the society that permits women and men to mingle freely, display themselves, and compete or allure one another through sexual attraction. These consequences are significant and cannot be ignored. To make women into sex objects for the pleasure of men is not liberation. In fact, it is a dehumanizing form of oppression rejected by Islam. The liberation of the Muslim woman is that she is recognized by the content of her character rather than by the display of her physical attributes. From the Islamic point of view, "liberated" Western women — who must often worry about their looks, figure, and youth for the pleasure of others — are trapped in a form of slavery.

16. WOMEN IN ISLAM

Women and men are equal before God. Both are accountable before God. They equally receive their reward in the Hereafter for their faith and good deeds.

Marriage is strongly encouraged and is both a legal agreement and a sacred bond. Islam sees every woman, married or unmarried, as an individual in her own right. She has the same right to own property, earn wealth and spend it as a man has. Her wealth does not become the property of her husband after marriage or divorce. A woman has the right to choose whom she marries and, when married, does not change her last name, out of respect for her lineage. A woman can seek divorce if her marriage does not work out.

Economically, each man and woman is an independent legal entity. Men and women have the right to own their individual property, engage in business, and inherit from others. Both have the equal right to receive an education and to enter into gainful employment, as long as Islamic principles are not violated.

Seeking knowledge is the obligation of every Muslim, male or female. The type of knowledge that is most emphasized is religious knowledge. It is also required within a society to have professionals of both genders available for the benefit of the public. For example, society requires doctors, teachers, counselors, social workers, and many other important vocations. When there is a shortage of qualified personnel, it may become obligatory for women or men to gain expertise in these fields to fulfill the needs of the Muslim community. In this situation, the guidelines of Islam are to be upheld.

Women are encouraged to seek Islamic knowledge, pursue their academic endeavors within the framework of Islam, and strive to fulfill their intellectual curiosity. To prevent anyone from getting an education is contrary to the teachings of Islam.

A man is responsible for maintaining and protecting his family and providing the basic needs such as food, clothing, and shelter for his wife, children, and (if needed) other female relatives in the household. Women are not primarily responsible for this, even if married. The Prophet Muhammad[p] said that the most perfect in faith among believers is he who is best in manners to his wife.

17. MALE CHAUVINISM AND THE MUSLIM WORLD

Many people perceive Islam as a chauvinistic religion that belittles women. They cite the condition of women in some "Muslim countries" to prove this point.[19] Their mistake is that they fail to separate the culture of a given people from the true teachings of the religion they may profess. It is appalling that today the oppression of women still exists in many cultures around the world. Women in many Third World countries live horrible lives. They are dominated by men and denied many basic human rights. This does not apply to Muslim countries alone, nor does it apply to all Muslim countries. Islam condemns this oppression. It is a tragic injustice to blame these cultural practices on religious beliefs when the teachings of the religion do not call for such behavior. The teachings of Islam forbid the oppression of women and clearly emphasize that men and women are to be respected equally.

Unfortunately, oppressive practices against women that exist in certain parts of the world have mistakenly been associated with Islam by some people. One of these practices is the ancient pagan custom of female genital mutilation, sometimes mistakenly called female circumcision, which originated and is still practiced in the Nile River Valley and surrounding areas. It is practiced by a number of ethnic groups of a wide variety of faiths throughout parts of Africa, especially in northeastern Africa. Many women in Africa are victims of this horrible, dismembering, barbaric custom.

Female genital mutilation is an abomination and is absolutely forbidden in Islam. It is unfortunate that, even though Islam forbids it, certain ethnic groups have perpetuated this practice even after their acceptance of Islam, leading some to assume that it is a part of Islam. Today, as these people gradually gain a better understanding of Islam, they are abandoning this cruel pagan practice. In Kenya, for example, one group of people who do **not** practice female genital mutilation are the Muslims.

Male circumcision, however, is clearly an Islamic practice and in fact was taught by God's Prophets and Messengers, including the Prophet Abraham[p]. There should be no confusion between the prohibited act of female genital mutilation and the encouraged act of male circumcision.

Another horrible practice is that of "honor killing," when a man kills a female relative in his family because he feels disgraced and humiliated by her behavior. This conduct, although extremely rare, is practiced by certain groups of people in the Indian subcontinent, the Middle East, and other places. This is outright murder in Islam. It is not permissible for a person to kill anyone out of some notion of "honor." It is by no

---

19   Unfortunately, an "Islamic country," does not necessarily mean that the country's government or the people are following Islamic law (Shari'a).

means exclusive to Muslims and "Islamic countries," and it violates Islamic law. Racism, sexism, and all forms of bigotry or prejudice are also prohibited in Islam.

Unfortunately, forced marriage is practiced in many traditional societies. It is another practice that is forbidden in Islam. Some fathers had forced their daughters into marriage at the time of the Prophet Muhammad^p. When the women complained to the Prophet^p of this, he nullified their marriages or gave them the option of ending the marriage even if it had already been consummated, establishing the clear precedent for Islamic law concerning freedom of choice about marriage and putting an end to this oppressive practice. Sadly, this still goes on in many parts of the world today, including in a number of "Islamic countries." Although this practice is illegal in almost all countries, many women in traditional societies either do not know their rights or are too afraid to demand them.

All of these practices are against Islamic law, and it is the responsibility of all Muslims to eradicate them in their societies. Yes, Islam is tolerant of cultural diversity and does not believe in eradicating the ways of life of different people, nor does it force people to give up their cultural identity when they embrace Islam. However, when the cultural practices of a people contravene the laws of Islam or deprive people of their God-given, inalienable rights and freedom of choice, it becomes a religious **obligation** to abandon those practices.

18. ISLAM, WARFARE, AND JIHAD

The Qur'an makes it clear that it is permissible for people to fight back against those who attack them. God says, "*Fight in the cause of God those who fight you, but do not transgress limits; for God loves not transgressors.*" [Qur'an 2:190]

God says, "*And why should you not fight in the cause of God and of those who, being weak, are ill-treated [and oppressed]? Men, women, and children, whose cry is: 'Our Lord! Rescue us from this town, whose people are oppressors, and raise for us from You one who will protect; and raise for us from You one who will help.'*" [Qur'an 4:75]

The Qur'an also makes it clear that when the other party refrains from aggression, it is not permissible to attack them. God says, "*But if they cease, God is Oft-Forgiving, Most Merciful. And fight them on until there is no more tumult or oppression and there prevail justice and faith in God. But if they cease, let there be no hostility except to those who practice oppression.*" [Qur'an 2:192 – 193]

It is permissible to fight against oppression and persecution. This does not apply only to Islam and Muslims, because everyone has the right to worship God. God says, "*To those against whom war is made, permission is given [to fight] because they are wronged and verily God is Most Powerful for their aid. [They are] those who have been expelled from their homes in defiance of right [for no cause] except that they say, 'Our Lord is God.' If God did not check one set of people by means of another, there would surely have been pulled down monasteries, churches, synagogues, and mosques, in which the name of God is commemorated in abundant measure*" [Qur'an 22:39 – 40] This clearly means that Muslims must fight to protect and defend people of other faiths if they are in areas where the Muslims have effective power. The life, honor, and property of all people are considered sacred whether they are Muslim or not. All people must be free to worship God. **They must be free to make their own choices**. God *The Guardian of Faith*, explicitly says, "***There is no compulsion in religion.***" [Qur'an 2:256]

This brings us to the concept of jihad. The word **jihad literally means struggle** or exert effort, and applies to any colossal effort, not just to warfare. Jihad may even be to refrain from fighting or to resist one's own desires or evil inclinations. Even making peace could be jihad. **There is no such thing as "holy war" in Islam or in the Qur'an.** This is a mistranslation of the word. Holy war is carried out to forcibly subject others to one's religious beliefs. This is expressly forbidden in Islam.

Fighting in war can be jihad, but under what conditions? Muslims fight in defense, but so do others. What makes such fighting a jihad? The answer is that fighting only becomes jihad if it is for the sake of being obedient to God and in accordance with His divine law. It is not jihad to fight for wealth, nationalism, territory, honor, race, and so on. Jihad has a strong element of self-restraint not seen in any other forms of warfare. Even fighting against people who attacked first would not be jihad if the Muslims were to strike back in revenge.

In the life of the Prophet Muhammad[P], we have a practical example of how jihad is to be carried out. When Muhammad[P] began peacefully calling the people of Makkah to Islam, he was strongly opposed. Because of their belief, Muhammad[P] and his followers were severely persecuted, sanctioned, tortured, expelled, had their property seized, and were even killed. Despite all this, Muslims did not waver from the Islamic principles of peace, nonviolence, and passive resistance. After Muhammad[P] peacefully taught Islam for ten years, several Makkan chiefs and leaders formed an alliance, collaborating on a plot to secretly assassinate the Prophet[P] of God. The angel Gabriel informed Muhammad[P] of their assassination plot. On the night the assassination was to take place, Muhammad[P] fled Makkah for Medina, and was pursued closely by the assassins for days.[20] The situation grew continuously worse until the Muslims were forced to migrate. They were openly invited to emigrate to Medina, a city to the north, where Muhammad[P] was jubilantly welcomed as the Messenger of God and the leader. In Medina, the Islamic community was established, and from there the Prophet Muhammad[P] continued his peaceful mission of calling the people to Islam.

The Makkan alliance was intent on extinguishing Islam, Muhammad[P], and his monotheistic teachings. Several major military campaigns were waged by the Makkan army to attack Medina in order to annihilate Muslims. When the well-equipped armies of aggressors were forming on the horizon, far outnumbering the Muslims, God *The Wise*, gave Muslims permission for the first time to bear arms in defense of their life and faith in jihad. The pagan armies of Makkah were defeated by Muslims who were far inferior in numbers and equipment though blessed with faith.

After the Makkan alliance recognized that war was futile, Muslims initiated a nonaggression treaty which was signed between the Makkan alliance chiefs and the Prophet Muhammad[P]. Muslims are required by God to strive toward peace at any opportunity. This treaty allowed unarmed Muslims to perform the pilgrimage to the Ka'bah, built by Abraham[P]. This peaceful period proved discouraging to Makkan leaders who saw Muslim numbers grow rapidly. Masterminding another treacherous plot, the Makkan alliance attacked and slaughtered many in betrayal of the treaty with the Muslims, in order to put a stop to Islam and peace. It was only after the Makkan alliance violated the treaty, that the Qur'anic verse ordering Muslims to jihad against this tyranny was revealed. Amazingly the Makkans did not engage in combat. Muhammad[P] entered Makkah humbly, and instead of taking revenge, he offered general amnesty and forgiveness to everyone. Muslims **peacefully** conquered Makkah without bloodshed, cleansing the Ka'bah and destroying all the idols. Muhammad[P]

---

20   This journey made by Muhammad[P] is known as the hijra, which marks the start of the Islamic calendar. The Islamic calendar consists of twelve months. Each month begins with the sighting of the new crescent moon. This practice is similar to the original Hebrew calendar that also had twelve lunar months with the same reckoning.

forbade any oppression, injustice, or compulsion in religion and did not allow any doors to be forced open. He graciously forgave his most bitter enemies, including those who had severely persecuted him and had even killed members of his family. This is Muhammad[p], a true example of Islam, the pinnacle of humanity, and the clear example of jihad.

The following will further clarify how fighting in Islam was conducted. The Prophet Muhammad[p] forbade the killing of any noncombatants. Ibn 'Umar, a companion of the Prophet[p] said, "I saw the body of a slain woman during one of the battles of the Prophet[p], so he forbade the killing of women and children." [Book of Al-Bukhari and Muslim]

Rabah b. Rabi was another companion of the Prophet Muhammad[p]. He gave the following account of an incident that occurred during one of the battles: "We were with God's Messenger[p] during a battle and we saw people gathered together. He dispatched a man to find out why they were gathered. The man returned and said: 'They are gathered around a slain woman.' So God's Messenger[p] said: 'She should not have been attacked!' Khalid b. al-Walid was leading the forces, so he dispatched a man to him saying: 'Tell Khalid not to kill women or laborers [civilians].'" [Book of Sunan Abi Dawud]

God's Messenger[p] used to say the following words to his troops before sending them to fight: "Go forward in the name of God. Do not kill an elderly person, nor a child, nor a woman, and do not exceed the bounds." [Book of Muwatta']

From all of this it is easy to see the position of Islam on terrorism. **Terrorism is against Islamic principles**. Terrorism is a form of warfare in which innocent people are specifically targeted in order to instill fear in a society. It is clear from the preceding that even during war, when the Muslims are defending against an aggressive enemy, they are never allowed to target any civilians, or to destroy crops, trees, or livestock. This is strictly prohibited by Islamic law and the clear examples of the Prophet Muhammad[p]. The killing of innocents is murder and a crime against God and humanity, **even during times of war and even when the other side does not similarly respect civilian life**. One who intentionally kills innocent people is a murderer who deserves the punishment for murder. Terrorism is categorically prohibited in Islam and Islamic law rejects the premise that a non-legitimate tactic can ever lead to a positive result.

Throughout Islamic history, the behavior of Muslims who followed the Qur'an and the Sunnah of the Prophet Muhammad[p], as well as how they treated others in times of war, has been exemplary. Abu Bakr, a companion of the Prophet Muhammad[p] and the first Caliph (successor and leader) who came after him, sent an army to Syria to fight the aggressive Roman legions and went out to give them words of encouragement. He said: "You are going to find a group of people who have devoted themselves to the worship of God [i.e., monks], so leave them to what they are doing."

When Umar, a companion of the Prophet Muhammad[p] and the second Caliph, drove the Roman legions out of Jerusalem, the Muslims were welcomed as liberators. Even though the Muslims had conquered the land, they were not allowed to look upon the inhabitants of the land as their enemies. Their enemies were only the Roman legions who had aggressed against them. When Umar entered Jerusalem as a conqueror, he came humbly. Instead of dictating harsh terms to the people, he brought a treaty that guaranteed the people of Jerusalem, who were predominantly Christian, their safety and freedom from all persecution. The following is from the treaty that he drafted for them:

"This is what Umar, the commander of the faithful, grants to the people in peace. He grants them the safety of their persons, their churches, and their crosses… their churches will not be shut down nor destroyed. Nothing will be taken from them or from their crosses. They will not be compelled to abandon their faith nor shall any one of them be abused."

To reiterate, there is no such thing as a "holy war" in Islam. War is atrocious and can never be holy. Muslims are not allowed to force their religion on anyone. The word jihad means "struggle." This struggle can be of a military nature. When it is, the difference between jihad and war becomes clear. Jihad can never be fought for worldly gain, for conquest, or for revenge. Muslims must fight to protect the freedom of the people to worship God when that freedom is forcibly attacked. They are never allowed to attack innocent people, even when they are themselves attacked.

Any people who go against this established principle of Islamic law are fighting in contradiction to Islamic principles. It is ludicrous for anyone to call this fighting a jihad, a word that means striving for the cause of Islam. In general, they are murderers in the light of Islamic law and should be treated as such.

19. SCIENCE AND TECHNOLOGY

One of the hallmarks of Islam is its complete harmony with science. A Muslim considers conflict between scientific facts and religion to be impossible. Religion comes from God, *The First* and *The Last*, and so does the universe that He alone created. It is impossible for one to contradict the other.

A Muslim assumes that a natural explanation can be found for everything in God's creation — from the formation of the stars and galaxies to the origin and diversity of different species. A Muslim should never rely on miracles to explain natural phenomena. A Muslim believes that miracles are instances where God contravenes His own natural laws for a specific reason, such as to assist one of His Prophets or to answer a prayer. Miraculous explanations should never be resorted to in order to explain something in the natural world or to cover up human ignorance on a scientific matter.

There has never been a scientific fact or a valid scientific theory that contradicted the teachings of Islam. Whatever science uncovers, it only increases our knowledge of God's magnificent creation. This is why Islam actively encourages scientific endeavors and why the Qur'an commands us to study God's signs in nature. In fact, the Qur'an has many amazing scientific references, that with the help of today's modern technological advancements, are just recently becoming fully understood.

Islam also allows us to fully enjoy the fruits of human ingenuity. We are encouraged to strive to better the world. Islam welcomes technological advances. Technology can be employed for good or evil. Technology itself is neutral. It is our responsibility to use the knowledge that God has blessed us with for the betterment of all humanity.

In the early days of Islam, when people adhered to its beliefs and principles, there was a flowering of science, culture, trade, and technology. Scholars in the Islamic world researched and advanced the fields of mathematics, chemistry, physics, medicine, astronomy, architecture, art, literature, geography, history, and more. Muslim scientists invented the magnetic compass, the astrolabe, and the clock pendulum, to name a few. Many critical systems such as algebra, the Arabic numerals (which are the same numbers that we currently use), and the very concept of zero (vital to the advancement of mathematics) were introduced to medieval Europe through Muslim scholars. The teachings of Islam brought about this scientific awareness, which eventually ignited and propelled the European Renaissance. It was only after people began deviating from the simple original Islamic principles and beliefs that the advancements and scientific achievements of the Muslim world began to cease and fall into obscurity.

20. FUNDAMENTALISM AND TERRORISM

Fundamentalism comes from the root word fundare, which means "a base or foundation." The definition of fundamentalism in reference to religion is "religious beliefs based on a literal interpretation of a religious text."

If you ask a Westerner, "What is the first image that comes to mind when you hear the word 'Muslim'?" many answer, "Terrorist." This may be due to the fact that the word Muslim is often paired with the word "terrorist" in the media. If a Jew or Christian were to take part in an act that is clearly considered terrorism, one would not hear that person called a "Christian terrorist" or a "Jewish terrorist." Just as Jim Jones (who claimed to represent Christ) is not considered representative of Christianity, terrorists should not be considered representatives of Islam.

Two phrases often used interchangeably are "Muslim terrorist" and "Muslim fundamentalist." "Muslim terrorist" is an oxymoron; **one who truly practices Islam cannot be a terrorist**. And if we were to refer to the definition of fundamentalism, we would know that these two phrases are mistakenly or intentionally being used interchangeably, and that they actually have opposite meanings. A true Islamic fundamentalist is one who strictly adheres to the fundamentals of Islam, which can only be defined by the Qur'an and the life and teachings of the Prophet Muhammad[p]. This is the **opposite** of what people commonly call "Islamic fundamentalism." Within true Islamic fundamentalism one would **never** see crimes against humanity, heinous acts of hatred, political killing, terrorism, oppression, religious extremism or zealotry, or the forcing of one's religion on others. All of these acts are clearly forbidden in Islam. Muhammad[p] was a pinnacle of humanity's generosity and compassion.

When it comes to the media, the spotlight is shining on dramatic murderers who are repeatedly referred to as "Islamic fundamentalists." This is in total contradiction to the definition of the **truly** practicing Muslim fundamentalists. It is a tragedy that many people have an enormous and unfounded fear of Islam and what is mistakenly thought to be Islam's fundamental beliefs. From the time of the Crusades, there are still some people who have taken an aggressively hostile and demonizing stance toward Islam.

It is distressing when one reads a newspaper article or hears a broadcast report that takes quotations from the Qur'an out of context to create fear or divisiveness.[21] Misrepresenting or twisting any religious text is despicable, whether it is done by "terrorists" or by "evangelists." Fear mongers who misrepresent religious principles to create alienation, fear, and hatred are another type of terrorist. Terrorism can be physical, emotional, or psychological. At the very least, it is the duty of all people who wish to counter any kind of terrorism to become informed about one another's true beliefs. Unfortunately, polarizing propaganda has been relentlessly spun into the sensationalism of today's media, unjustly fueled by the fear of this "unknown and strange" faith. Today's mass media, which is controlled by few, appears to be the most researched, refined, and powerful mind-control instrument ever devised by man to shape "world opinion." Alienation is escalating. It often seems that all governments need enemies to fuel the military and to bring about "national unity." During the Cold

---

21   In Matthew 10:34, Jesus[p] is quoted as saying, "Do not think that I have come to bring peace on earth; I have not come to bring peace but a sword." This illustrates the danger of taking a quotation out of context without understanding the broader, noble, and beautiful message of Jesus[p]. Those who wish to defame any religion by cutting, pasting, and twisting any religious texts, sadly, may achieve their evil purpose.

War, "the enemy" was "Communism." Today, Muslims globally often find themselves in the cross hairs, cast as "the enemy."

Unfortunately, across the globe those Muslims who are practicing true Islamic principles are becoming an "endangered species." As Muslims struggle to practice their beliefs many are challenged, not only by their own government or Western governments, but they also find themselves caught between secularists and narrow-minded extremists. The subjective corporate media spotlight is not shining on the **true** Islamic fundamentalists.

Pressure Cooker: Today there are millions of people living under great oppression. Their future looks hopeless as their families and homes are being crushed by humiliating injustice and violence. When such conditions are ignored or viewed with callous indifference by the rest of the world, it can and does produce a desperate rage that transcends all culture and religion. These are the conditions in which many Muslims find themselves today. Lacking hope and having lost patience with the dysfunctional options placed before them, they seek relief or justice in desperation. Thus we are seeing more and more of them willing to take extreme measures, willing to react in violent ways, even to kill themselves, in order to deliver a militant or political act of defiance. Committing suicide and killing civilians are both forbidden in Islam. Those living in the Muslim world who are in this "pressure cooker" of oppression may seek any nonreligious or religious justification for their desperate, violent, and extreme actions. If they look long enough, they sometimes find what they are looking for, as there are people of an extreme mindset in every religion who do not truly practice and represent the actual tenets of their faith.

21. SUMMARY

Islam is… a religion of justice, peace, mercy, and forgiveness, a faith which is often misunderstood and misrepresented. **Islam means to surrender one's will to God**, *The Peace*. Islam is the way of life for anyone who chooses to accept that **there is one God only, and none is worthy of worship but Him**. This world is temporary and no more than a trial for humanity, after which we will all die and return to God, *The Taker*. The life of the Hereafter is forever. God, *The Light*, for the guidance of the children of Adam[p], sent us Prophets: Abraham[p], Moses[p], Jesus[p], Muhammad[p], all Prophets of Islam. God chose Muhammad[p] as His final Prophet and Messenger and honored him with the privilege of revealing the Qur'an through him. The Qur'an is the direct unalterable word of God, not the word of Muhammad[p], who was an unlettered man. God has preserved the Qur'an with its teachings for all of humanity.

The five fundamental acts of worship for Muslims are as follows:

1. To "**testify that there is no deity except God, and that Muhammad is His Messenger**" *2.* To **pray** five times a day *3.* To pay the yearly **alms** *4.* To **fast** during Ramadan *5.* To make the **pilgrimage** to Makkah.

It is imperative to understand jihad. Jihad is a struggle for the cause of God alone and cannot violate Islamic principles. Terrorism is clearly rejected by Islam and can never be called jihad. God states that there is no compulsion in religion. Human rights and freedom of choice are sacred. In Islam, women play a very important role. Women are equal to and required to be honored by men.

God mentions in the Qur'an that He has perfected Islam as a religion for all of humanity, thus completing His favor upon us. God has prepared for us the light of Islam as a guide for humanity's return to Him.

22. EDITOR'S NOTE

We are told by scientists that space contains over 120 billion galaxies. We know that every one of us was created by God *The Most Magnificent*, from a single cell. When I think about this, I can't help but be humbled and realize my extreme insignificance in the light of God's amazing splendor. Satan swore to deceive humanity, to bring us misunderstanding, animosity, hatred, and war. To do my part in opposing Satan, my motives are to please my Lord by promoting peace through understanding.

Life is short and precious; it is tragic to waste it by piling up temporal material gain while ignoring the true purpose of creation: **to worship God alone**. Many people spend their precious lives accumulating temporal material wealth. Through Islam, God invites us to turn to that which is everlasting, eternal. On the Day of Judgment, we will be accountable for what we knew and how we had applied it. We will be asked about our worship. Now is the time for us to prepare for the answer.

This book is based on the lectures I have been giving on Islam for the past two decades. It would not have been possible without God's mercy and the help and assistance of my brothers and sisters. I thank you, my readers, for your time and interest in understanding Islam, the faith of one-fifth of the world's population. For additional information on Islam you can contact us by visiting www.islam-is.com. We also welcome your questions as well as your comments and feedback for consideration in this ongoing work. I invite you to share any or all of this material. I ask only that you do not quote this information out of context.

Please forgive me if in this work I have offended anyone. Because of my passion for Islam, I express my faith strongly. I greatly value individual choice and respect differences. **Understanding and justice are the way to peace**, and because Islam is often perceived in the West as a religion of narrow-minded zealots out to convert the world by force, I feel it is vital that I convey my faith in clear and unambiguous language to counter misconceptions.

May God bless us all with guidance. Any good that comes from this work is by God's benevolence, and if I have said anything unhelpful, it is my shortcoming. God, *The Exalted* and *The Loving*, is perfect.

"Oh, *The All Hearing*, protect us from all evil and guide us to the truth."

Peace be upon you,

Pete Seda

ISBN 0-9719158-0-6

50300

9 780971 915800

Printed in U.S.A. $3.00